THE PRIVATE EAR

A Play in One Act

by

PETER SHAFFER

SAMUEL FRENCH

LONDON
NEW YORK TORONTO SYDNEY HOLLYWOOD

GB 573 02215 1

THE PRIVATE EAR

Produced together with *The Public Eye* by H. M. Tennent
Ltd at the Globe Theatre, London, on the 10th May 1962,
with the following cast of characters:

(in the order of their appearance)

TED	*Douglas Livingstone*
BOB	*Terry Scully*
DOREEN	*Maggie Smith*

Directed by PETER WOOD

Décor by RICHARD NEGRI

*The action of the Play passes in Bob's bed-sitting-room
in Belsize Park, on a summer evening*

Time—the present

THE PRIVATE EAR

SCENE—*Bob's bed-sitting-room in Belsize Park. A summer evening.*

It is a fairly shabby attic room. The door to the stairs and entrance is down L. *In the corner up* L *there is a small kitchen which can be closed off with a sliding door at the downstage side. In the living-room there is a dormer window at the back, looking out over a grimy roofscape, and an area of sky. It opens french-window fashion and leading on to a small flat roof, bounded by a low wall. The kitchen has two windows, one in the back wall overlooking the roof and another in the wall separating it from the living-room. In the living-room there is a bed up* R, *made up as a sofa, a chest of drawers with a mirror on it,* R, *and down* R *some shelves with books and a large rack of gramophone records. Above the bed hangs a large print of Botticelli's "Birth of Venus". The back wall,* L *of the window is used as a wardrobe and is screened off by curtains. There is a small dining-table* LC, *with a wooden armchair above it and an upright chair* L *of it. A leather-covered armchair stands* RC *and there is a stool down* C. *Under the window up* C *there is a rough box used as a step when going out to the flat roof beyond. Most noticeable are the large, twin speakers of a stereophonic gramophone. The speakers are suspended from the sloping ceiling,* R *and* L *of the dormer window. The gramophone is down* R. *A large water storage cistern is on a shelf over the kitchen door. In the kitchen there is a sink and draining-board, a refrigerator, a gas stove, a small table and some dresser shelves.*

When the CURTAIN *rises, the stage is empty and in darkness. The noise of the water cistern can be heard. The* LIGHTS *come up. It is seven o'clock on a bright midsummer evening. The sun streams through the window.* TED *marches in down* L. *He is aged about twenty-five or six, cocky and extroverted, fitted out gaily by Shaftesbury Avenue. His whole relationship to Bob shows an air of patronizing domination. He wears his hat and sun-glasses, carries a small transistor in one hand and a bunch of sweet peas in the other. The transistor is playing. He goes up* C, *looks out of the window, does a few dance steps, removes his hat, puts it on the bed, goes to the dressing-table, looks in the mirror, straightens his hair then turns.*

TED (*calling*) Bob. (*He switches off the transistor*) Bob.
BOB (*off* L) Hello.
TED. I've arrived—and to prove it, I'm here! Where are you?
BOB. In the bathroom. What time is it?
TED. Ten past seven. What time is she coming? (*He puts the transistor in his pocket*)

(BOB *runs in down* L, *closing the door behind him. He is a not very prepossessing boy of twenty-one. He is wearing a dressing-gown over underclothes and carries a towel*)

BOB (*a North Country accent*) Half past. (*He goes to the table, takes a tablecloth and three mats from the table drawer, lays the cloth and sets out the mats*)
TED (*moving* C) Well, that's twenty minutes. You've got plenty of time. Just take it all nice and easy. I've bought you some flowers. Provides that chic touch to the décor you're a tiny bit in need of.
BOB. They're pretty. (*He goes into the kitchen and returns with a tray with paper napkins, glasses, water jug and cutlery*)
TED. You know, you ought to be flattered I'm here to-night playing cook for you. Do you know where I could have been? (*He takes out a photograph*) With her. How about them for a pair of Bristols?

(BOB *puts the tray on the chair* L *of the table, crosses to Ted and takes the photograph*)

(*He removes his sun-glasses and puts them in his breast pocket*) And that hair. It's what they call raven black. It's got tints of blue in it. Lustrous, as the ad says. You can't keep your hands off it. See the way she holds herself? (*He takes the photograph from Bob*) That's what they used to call carriage, my boy.

(BOB *moves to the bed, puts the towel on it, picks up his trousers from the bed and puts them on*)

Carriage. You don't see any carriage nowadays. Just fiddle and wiggle, that's all. 'Course, most of the girls you meet think they've got it—poor little nits. Toddling about on stilettos making holes in the lino. Carriage! Look at her. Miss Carriage.

BOB (*moving above the table*) Where did you meet her?

TED. Up the *Mecca* last night, twisting herself giddy with some little nit. I sort of detached her. She wanted a date for tonight, but I said: "Sorry, girl, no can do tomorrow. I'm engaged for one night only as chef to my mate Tchaik, who is entertaining a bird of his own. Very special occasion." So you be grateful. Greater love hath no man than to pass up a bird like this for his mate. (*He puts the photograph on the table and crosses to* R)

BOB (*picking up the photograph*) What's her name?

TED. You won't believe it if I tell you. Lavinia. Honest. Lavinia. How's that for a sniff of class? The rest of it's not so good. Beamish. Lavinia Beamish. (*He takes the tissue paper from the flowers and picks up a small vase from the chest of drawers*)

BOB. She's beautiful.

TED. Do you think so?

BOB. I do—yes.

TED. She's going to go off fairly quickish, though. (*He puts the paper in the waste-paper basket up* C) In three years she'll be all lumpy like old porridge.

BOB. I don't know how you do it. I don't, really. (*He puts the photograph on the table then lays out the cutlery, etc.*)

TED. Just don't promise them anything, that's all. (*He moves to* R *of the table*) Make no promises, they can't hang anything on you, can they?

BOB. I wouldn't know. I really am, by the way.

TED. What?

BOB. Grateful.

TED (*putting the flowers in the vase*) Oh, forget it. It's only a bird, isn't it? (*He picks up the jug of water from the table*) Here, I heard a good one yesterday. The Tate Gallery just paid ten thousand pounds for a picture of a woman with five breasts. D'you know what it's called? (*He pours water into the vase*)

BOB. What?

TED. "Sanctity." (*He replaces the jug on the table*)

BOB (*not understanding*) Sanctity?

Ted. *Un, deux, trois, quatre, cinq,* titty. Come on, let's get on with din, then. Half past, you say? (*He puts the vase on the table then goes into the kitchen*)

Bob. Quarter of an hour. That's if she comes at all. (*He takes his clean shirt from the line up* c, *removes his dressing-gown and dons the shirt*)

(Ted *comes from the kitchen with a salt cellar*)

Ted. Of course she'll come. Why shouldn't she? It's a free dinner, isn't it? (*He moves to the table, puts down the salt cellar and stares at the cutlery*) Well, for God's sake! Is that what you call laying a table?

Bob (*anxiously*) What's wrong with it?

Ted. It'd be great for the chimpanzees' tea-party. (*He points to the place settings*) This one's got three knives, and this one's got three spoons. Well done.

Bob (*hurrying to the table*) Oh, Lord! (*He reaches out to rearrange the cutlery and upsets the vase*)

Ted. You're in a state, aren't you? (*He picks up the vase*) Well, get a cloth.

(Bob *moves up* c, *collects a teacloth from the wall outside the window, returns to the table and mops it*)

(*He picks up the photograph*) You've wet my Lavinia. I'll have to dry you out, luv. (*He crosses to the chest of drawers*) Tchaik's in a state. Pit-a-pat, isn't it? Pit-a-flippin'-pat. (*He sticks the photograph in the mirror and turns*) Look, what's up? It's just a girl, isn't it?

Bob. Yes.

Ted. Well, then. What's so special? (*He moves to the table*)

Bob. Nothing.

Ted. All right. So she looks like a Greek goddess. (*He takes the cloth from Bob and goes into the kitchen*)

Bob. Look, Ted, I didn't say that. I just said her neck reminded me . . . (*He gets his raincoat from the armchair, takes a bottle of wine from the pocket, places the bottle on the table, then moves to the wardrobe up* lc)

Ted (*coming from the kitchen*) All right, her neck. (*He picks up the bottle of wine*) What's this?

(BOB *hangs his raincoat in the wardrobe*)

BOB. It's called Rose. (*He pronounces it like the flower*) The man in the Victoria said it'd go well with the lamb chops.

(TED *holds up the bottle, drops it and catches it with his other hand*)

(*He runs to Ted with a cry*) Ted!

TED. Well, *he* didn't know what he was talking about, did he? Ignorant little nit.

BOB (*moving RC; alarmed*) What d'you mean?

(TED *backs Bob to the stool.* BOB *sits*)

TED. Look and learn, will you? This is a *Rosé*. It's a light French wine. You drink it by itself, not with heavy meat like lamb. Get it? For that you want a claret or burgundy. That's a Burgogna or a—well, or a claret. In any case you've got to serve this cold, can't you read? "*Servir legerement frappé.*" See? (*Pityingly*) He's quite hopeless. I'll put it in the fridge. (*He goes into the kitchen and puts the bottle in the refrigerator*)

BOB. Is it going to taste rotten, then?

(TED *picks up a filled carrier bag from the kitchen table and returns to the living-room*)

TED. Well, it depends on what you like, doesn't it? (*He puts the bag on the table*) Some people are happy with bottled cider or lovely limeade.

(BOB *looks worried*)

(*Seeing Bob's face*) Oh, don't worry. *She* won't know the difference, anyway. What do we start with?

BOB (*rising and moving to the table*) Soup. I got a tin of mushroom. (*He takes the tin from the bag*) It's quite good if you add milk.

TED. In a Works Canteen sort of way, I suppose. And what to follow?

BOB. Chops. Lamb. (*He takes three chops from the bag, they are in cellophane*) Do you have to unfreeze them first?

TED. They won't taste much, either way. Not out of those bins in the delly. They never do. You should always go to a proper butcher, mate. (*He inspects the chops*) A bit on the shaved side, aren't they?

BOB. They were the biggest they have.

TED. Well, just so long as I have that one. Let's hope *she's* got a genteel appetite. Probably will have. Most girls think it's not really posh to eat a lot. (*He takes a tin of peas from the bag*) These go with them?

BOB. Yes. Lamb and peas.

TED. You should have got petty pois—not these marrow-fats. It's more chic. You know, the little ones. The other size are sort of com.

BOB. They're not, are they?

TED. Definitely. Com. C.O.M. *She* won't know, mind you, but it's just the difference between class and no class, that's all.

BOB (*upset*) It's going to be a right fiasco, isn't it? I'd better open them. (*He takes the tin of peas and goes into the kitchen*)

TED. That's my job, isn't it?

BOB. I can do it. (*He picks up the opener, stands in the kitchen doorway and starts cutting away furiously at the tin*)

TED (*replacing the soup and chops in the carrier bag*) Now look, don't get rattled: that's the worst thing you can do. Not with that pit-a-pat going, anyway. It's probably a good thing, anyway, not to have too much fancy food. That way she'll take pity on you, think you're not eating right and all that palaver. Needs a wife's good cooking. You know. In your case it's bloody time.

(BOB *cuts his finger on the tin and cries out*)

BOB. Now look what I've done.

TED. Steady on. You really are in a state, aren't you? Put it under the tap for a moment.

BOB. There's a plaster in that drawer. (*He goes to the sink*)

TED (*moving to the chest of drawers*) Well, pull yourself together for God's sake. (*He takes a plaster from a box in the drawer*) You go on this way, the whole evening is going to be a flipping fiasco. You're not going to get far with any girl shaking blood over her cardigan. They're cowards that way. They can't stand the sight of blood on their woollies.

(BOB *comes from the kitchen and crosses to Ted*)

BOB. It's all right—just a nick.

TED. Give here. (*He puts the plaster on Bob's finger*) Now look, why don't you take yourself a snort and just sit down. I can cope in there. A gin and french, that's what you need.

BOB. There isn't any gin.

TED. I might have known. What are you going to give her first, then?

BOB. First?

TED. To drink.

BOB. Look, I said she had one drink. I didn't say she was a boozer, did I?

TED. You don't have to be a boozer to want a cocktail. It's the chic thing. No, it's not even chic. Even the suburbs do it. You can't ask *her* to sit down to eat just like that. You're really hopeless, aren't you?

BOB (*quietly, but with more firmness*) I asked you to help, you know. Not to make comments. (*He sits in the armchair, takes a pair of socks from the arm and puts one on. There is a large hole in it. He removes the sock, throws the pair on to the bed, rises, moves to the dressing-table and takes a clean pair of socks from the drawer*)

TED (*moving up* C) Well, help's one thing. This is just bricks out of straw, isn't it? (*He moves to R of the table*) Anyway, I didn't know I'd have to organize the whole bit. What's come over you? I know you've always been a bit on the twitch, but I've never seen you like this, all to pieces. What's she done to you? It's like the snake and the old guinea pig, isn't it? (*He puts finishing touches to the table*)

BOB (*sitting in the armchair*) Don't be daft.

TED (*turning to him*) Are you really serious, Tchaik?

BOB (*avoiding Ted's eye*) About what? (*He puts on the socks*)

TED. This girl.

BOB. How can I be serious about someone I met for a few minutes?

TED. Well, I never know with you. You're deep. It's all that Celtic Twilight in your blood. That's not original, by the way. Miss Story said it in the office last week. She said you were full of Celtic Twilight.

BOB (*removing his slippers*) Who's Miss Story? (*He puts on his shoes*)

TED. You know—the old bag in accounts. She said you were mystic.

BOB. Yes, I'm sure. (*He struggles with his laces*)

TED. Seriously, is there anything?

BOB. I told you, don't be daft. Why should there be?

TED (*tying Bob's laces for him*) Well, it's not every day you invite a girl to dinner, is it? Let's be honest. You go to hundreds of concerts, but you don't usually pick up a girl and invite her home for the old chops and vino, do you? So what gives?

BOB. I told you. We were next to each other.

TED. Yes?

BOB. I'd been watching her for ages out of the corner of my eye. She was absolutely beautiful. I couldn't believe it when she dropped her programme.

TED. Well, that was a piece of luck for you, wasn't it? Of course you handed it back with a mannerly bow?

BOB. I didn't, as a matter of fact. I didn't like to—in case she thought anything. It just lay there between us for about ten minutes. And then it was the interval, and I had to make up my mind. She was just going out when I picked it up and gave it her.

TED. And then what happened?

BOB. She said: "Thank you."

TED. Original.

BOB. Well, I asked her if she liked music, and she said, "Yes". It was a daft question, really, I suppose. I mean, she wouldn't have been there otherwise, would she? In the end it turned out she was on her own, and I asked her if she'd have a coffee with me after. I could hardly believe my ears when she said "Yes".

TED. Why not? Even goddesses get thirsty. So?

BOB. So we went to an Espresso in South Ken.

TED. And held hands over two flat whites?

BOB. Not exactly, no. As a matter of fact, I couldn't think of very much to say to her. We were out in the street again inside of ten minutes.

TED. So that's why you asked me tonight? To help out with the talk?

Bob. I suppose, yes.

Ted. I really am flattered. (*He moves above the table*) Your first date with her and you invite me along, too.

Bob. Well, you know what to say to women. You've had the practice, haven't you?

Ted. There's no practice needed. You just say the first thing that comes into your head, as long as it's not dirt, of course. They don't much like dirt, though they'll go for that, too, if you present it right You know—with a man-of-the-world smile.

Bob. If I tried anything like that, I'd look like a seducer in a silent film.

Ted (*going into the kitchen*) Well, you'd have to find your own style, of course. The important thing is, you've taken the plunge. You've invited a girl home. (*He removes his jacket and hangs it in the kitchen*)

Bob. Oh, I had to, in this case. There's no question about that. She was . . .

Ted. What? (*He picks up the tea-towel and tucks it round his waist as an apron*)

Bob. You'll laugh.

Ted. No, I won't. Go on. Well?

Bob. Well, the first girl I ever saw I wanted to see again. I mean, had to. She's got a look about her—not how people are, but how they ought to be.

Ted (*coming into the room*) Steady.

Bob. No, I mean it. When I said her neck reminded me, you know what I was thinking of? (*He rises and moves c*)

Ted. Who?

Bob (*indicating the print on the wall behind the bed*) Her.

Ted. Venus?

Bob. Yes. Botticelli would have been proud to paint her. She's got exactly the same neck—long and gentle. (*He moves to the picture*) That's a sign.

Ted. A sign?

Bob. Yes.

Ted. What for?

Bob. Spiritual beauty. Like Venus. That's what this picture really represents. The birth of beauty in the human soul. My Botticelli book says so. (*He moves to the shelves down R and snatches up a Fontana Pocket Library edition, opens it and reads*) Listen. "Venus, that is to say Humanity, is a nymph of excellent comeliness, born of heaven. Her soul and mind are Love and Charity. Her eyes, dignity. Her hands, liberality. Her feet, modesty." All signs, you see. (*He reads*) "Venus is the Mother of Grace, of Beauty, and of Faith."

TED. And your bird's the mum of all that?

BOB (*replacing the book*) No, of course not. I'm not a fool. But that look of hers is ideal beauty, Ted. It means she's got grace inside her. Really beautiful people are beautiful inside. Don't you see? (*He takes his tie from the chest of drawers, and puts it on*)

TED. You mean like after Andrews Liver Salts?

BOB. That's exactly what I mean.

TED. Oh, Tchaik, now seriously, come off it. I think that's daft. I mean it is, boy. (*He crosses to Bob*) There's a lot of stupid, greedy little nitty girls about who are as pretty as pictures.

BOB (*turning*) I don't mean pretty.

TED. Then what? (*He ties Bob's tie for him*)

BOB. Well, what you called carriage, for instance. What your Lavinia's got. It's not just something you learn, the way to walk and that. It's something inside you. I mean real carriage, the way you see some girls walk, sort of pulling the air round them like clothes. You can't practice that. You've got first to love the world. Then it comes out.

TED. I see. Have you got any red-currant jelly? They always serve it with lamb in chic restaurants.

BOB. I've got some jam.

TED. What kind?

BOB. Gooseberry.

(*The doorbell rings*)

There she is!

TED. So I hear. Calm down. All right, now listen. The last swallow of coffee and I'm away. Deadline at nine-thirty. Work to do at home. Got it? Nine-thirty you see me, nine-thirty-one you don't.

BOB (*moving to the wardrobe*) Look, it's not like that at all. (*He takes his jacket from the wardrobe*)

TED. No? Well, if it isn't, it ought to be. Go on, then,

Bob (*putting on his jacket*) Yes. The soup's in a tin. (*He moves down* L)

Ted. You showed me. (*He hurriedly picks up Bob's slippers, collects the dressing-gown and towel from the bed, bundles them into the wardrobe and closes the curtains. He then collects two cushions, puts them on the stool and sets the stool* R *of the table*)

Bob. Good.

(*The doorbell rings.* Bob *stands at a loss down* L)

Ted. Why not just leave her standing there? She'll go away in five minutes.

(Bob *turns to go*)

(*He shouts*) Hi! (*He runs to Bob, tears a cleaner's label from Bob's right sleeve then bites the tape from the back of the collar*) Go on! (*He gives Bob a push*)

Bob. I wish I had a drink to offer her.

Ted. Well, you haven't, have you?

(Bob *exits down* L.

Ted *crosses to the chest of drawers, tidies his hair, polishes his shoes on the back of his trouser legs, picks up the carrier bag and the tray, goes into the kitchen and closes the door.*

Bob *re-enters down* L *and stands aside.*

Doreen *enters down* L. *She is a pretty girl of about twenty, wearing an imitation ocelot coat. It is at once obvious that she is nervous also, and has no real pleasure in being there. Her reactions are anxious and tight, and these, of course, do nothing to reassure Bob*)

Doreen. I'm not too early?

Bob. No. Just right. (*He closes the door*) Actually, it's only just half past. You're very punctual.

Doreen. Unpunctuality's the thief of time, as my dad says.

Bob. To coin a phrase.

Doreen. Pardon?

Bob. Let me take your coat.

Doreen. Thank you. (*She slips her coat off. Under it she is wearing a dress and a cardigan*)

Bob (*taking the coat*) That's pretty.

Doreen. D'you like it?

BOB. I do, yes. Is it real? I mean—real leopard.

DOREEN. It's ocelot.

BOB (*hanging the coat on the hook behind the door down* L) Oh! (*He imitates Ted*) Very chic.

DOREEN. Pardon?

BOB. Won't you sit down.

DOREEN (*moving to* RC *and looking at the table laid for three*) Is this all yours? Or do you share?

BOB (*moving below the table*) No, I live alone. There's actually a friend here at the moment. He's helping with the dinner. We work in the same office.

DOREEN. Can I help?

BOB. No, it's all done. Really. All you can do is sit down and relax. (*With an attempt at "style", he gestures at the arm-chair*)

DOREEN. Thanks. (*She sits in the armchair*)

(*There is a tiny pause*)

BOB. Do you smoke?

DOREEN. I do a bit, yes.

BOB. Good! Tipped or plain? (*He crosses to the chest of drawers, picks up a cigarette box, opens it with a flourish and offers it to Doreen*)

DOREEN. Well! That's luxury for you, isn't it—both kinds. Tipped, thank you. (*She takes a cigarette*)

BOB. Allow me. (*He picks up a lighter from the chest of drawers and tries to snap it alight. It does not work. He fumbles with it, to no avail*)

DOREEN. It's all right, I've got a match. (*She takes matches from her handbag and lights her cigarette*)

(BOB *puts the lighter and cigarette box on the chest of drawers, crosses above Doreen and sits on the stool.* DOREEN *does not know what to do with her spent match and puts it in her handbag. There is a tiny pause*)

BOB. So, how have you been?

DOREEN. Fine. You?

BOB. Yes. Can't complain. Er—you're a typist, aren't you?

DOREEN. Stenographer. The place that trained me said: "Never call yourself a typist: it's lowering."

BOB. Oh. What kind of things do you—well, stenog, I suppose?

DOREEN. The usual letters.

BOB. Yours of the tenth?

DOREEN. Pardon?

BOB. "Dear sir, in reply to yours of the tenth . . ." Things like that?

DOREEN. Oh, I see. Yes, that's right. (laughs)

BOB. Do you mind it?

DOREEN. What?

BOB. Doing the same thing, day in, day out.

DOREEN. Well, there's not much choice, is there?

BOB. I suppose not.

DOREEN. You've got to earn your living, haven't you? Like my dad says, "It doesn't grow on trees."

BOB. No. Wouldn't they look odd if it did?

DOREEN. Pardon?

BOB. The trees.

DOREEN. Oh, yes. (*She looks nervously at him*)

BOB (*plunging on*) Like when people say unpunctuality's the thief of time—like your dad says.

(DOREEN *is at a loss with her cigarette ash*)

I always used to try and imagine unpunctuality in a mask —you know—with a sack labelled "swag". That's what comes of having a literal mind. (*He looks for something to supply as an ashtray, rises, crosses to the chest of drawers, takes the lid from the plaster box and hands it to Doreen*) I remember I had awful trouble at school one day with that poem which says, "The child is father of the man." I simply couldn't see it. I mean, how could a child be a father? (*He resumes his seat*) I couldn't get beyond that. I don't think imagination's a thing you can cultivate though, do you? I mean, you're either born with it or you're not.

DOREEN. Oh, yes, you're born with it.

BOB. Or you're not.

DOREEN. Yes.

BOB. There ought to be a sign so parents can tell. There probably is, if we knew how to read it. I mean, all babies are born with blue eyes, but no-one ever says there's a difference in the blue. And I bet there is. I bet if you looked really hard at six babies the first day they were born you'd see six different kinds of blue. Milky blue—sharp blue, you know, like cornflower colour—even petrol blue. And they each mean something different about characters. Of course, after the first day they all fade and become the same. It's a thought, anyway.

DOREEN. Oh, yes.

BOB. Daft one. Would you like a drink?

DOREEN. Well, I wouldn't say no.

BOB. Good! What would you like?

DOREEN. Whatever you suggest. I'm not fussy.

BOB. Gin and french?

DOREEN. That'd be lovely.

BOB (*rising and crossing to the chest of drawers*) Well, if you'll just excuse me. (*He picks up a Dimple Haig bottle and shakes out some sixpences into his hand*)

DOREEN. What are you doing?

BOB. I won't be a moment. (*He replaces the bottle*)

DOREEN. Can I help?

BOB (*crossing to the door down* L) I won't be a second.

DOREEN. Where are you going?

BOB. Just round the corner. To the pub. It's only a step away. (*He opens the door*)

DOREEN. Haven't you got any in?

BOB. No. I—(*inventing it*) I don't drink.

DOREEN (*rising*) You don't?

BOB. No.

DOREEN. Well, don't go on my account.

BOB. That's all right. I mean, I want to.

DOREEN. That's silly.

BOB. Why?

DOREEN. Because I don't drink, either. (*She resumes her seat*)

BOB. You're just saying that.

DOREEN. No, honest. I don't.

BOB. Ever?

DOREEN. Well, at Christmas and that. But I don't want one now. I only said it to be sociable.

BOB. You sure?

DOREEN. Positive.

BOB. Well, that's all right then. (*He closes the door and pockets the coins*)

DOREEN. Of course.

(*There is a pause*)

BOB (*fingering Doreen's coat*) You know, I always thought in ocelot was a bird.

DOREEN. Did you?

BOB. Yes. I must have been thinking of an ostrich.

(TED, *playing the waiter, enters from the kitchen with two glasses of wine on a tray*)

TED (*crossing to Doreen*) Cocktails, madame? A little chilled vino before din?

DOREEN (*delighted*) Ohh!

BOB. This is my friend, the one I told you about. Ted Veasey—Miss Marchant.

TED. Pleased to meet you.

DOREEN. How d'you do?

TED. Oh, *comme ci, comme ça*. You know, most people never answer that question—how do you do? That's because those who ask it don't really want to know. How do *you* do?

DOREEN. Oh, very nicely, thank you.

TED. That's all right, then. Do I have to call you "miss"?

DOREEN. Well, it is a bit formal, isn't it? Why don't you call me Doreen?

TED. Thanks. I will. If it's not too presumptuous. You see, I'm only the butler around here. (*He offers her a drink*) Mademoiselle?

DOREEN (*hesitating to take a drink*) Well . . .

BOB. I'm afraid she doesn't drink.

TED. No?

DOREEN. Well, only on special occasions.

TED. Well, tonight's an occasion, isn't it? Of course it is. A real proper—(*in French*) "occasion". Come on. Do you good.

DOREEN. Well—just to be sociable. (*She takes the drink*)

TED. That's it. (*He crosses to Bob and offers him the other drink*) Tchaik?

BOB. Well, you know *I* don't.

TED. Don't what?

BOB. Drink.

TED. Since when?

BOB (*unhappily*) Well, always ...

TED. First I've heard of it. You were sloshed last week.
(*To Doreen*) He was.

BOB. I mean, not before dinner.

TED. What?

BOB. Not on an empty stomach. You know I don't.

TED. Well, waste not, want not, I say. (*He drinks*) The
servants you get these days. See you, my dear, in two shakes
of a lamb's tale—or should I say, chop?

(TED *exits to the kitchen and closes the door*)

DOREEN. He's funny.

BOB. Yes, he is. He's marvellous to have in the office.
(*He crosses to* C) I mean, he's always cheerful.

DOREEN. Aren't you?

BOB (*sitting on the stool*) Not always, no.

DOREEN. What office do you work for?

BOB. Import-export. I'm just a glorified clerk, really.
At least that's what Ted keeps on telling me, and I suppose
he's right.

DOREEN. Why, is he over you?

BOB. In a way he is, yes.

DOREEN. What way?

BOB. Well, he's just been promoted to look after a small
department of his own. It means quite a bit of responsi-
bility. He's going to go a long way, I think. I mean he's
interested and keen—you know.

DOREEN. But aren't you?

BOB. Well, not so much as he is. He knows all about
economics. Tariffs and that. I'm afraid it's all rather
beyond me.

DOREEN. I like people who want to get on. Who've got
drive. That's something I respect. My dad's got drive.
That's one thing he has got.

BOB. What does he do?

DOREEN. Well, he's retired now. He used to be a Works'
Manager.

BOB. Where?

DOREEN. Edmonton.

BOB. Oh.

DOREEN. He says, if you haven't got drive, you might as well be dead.

BOB. He's probably right. Is that drink all right?

DOREEN. Yes, it's lovely.

BOB. Good.

DOREEN. Cheerio.

BOB. Cheerio. (*Enviously, he watches her drink*)

DOREEN. This is a nice room.

BOB. D'you like it?

DOREEN. Yes, I like large rooms.

BOB. So do I.

DOREEN. Most of the rooms you see today, they're tiny —like matchboxes.

BOB. Yes. (*He laughs obligingly, then rushes on eagerly*) Mind you, that would suit some people. I saw a man in the Tube yesterday who looked exactly like a safety match. Thin body like a stick, and a tiny black head. I remember thinking: Bryant and May could use you.

DOREEN. Pardon?

BOB. Bryant and May could use . . . (*He falls silent*)

(DOREEN *stares at him unencouragingly*)

(*Plunging on*) Mind you, it's not that large, really. Not when you have to eat and sleep all in the one. Still, it's hard finding places, and they're very tolerant here.

DOREEN. Tolerant?

BOB. I mean, they don't interfere with your private weaknesses—you know.

DOREEN. Pardon?

BOB. I mean your habits. I'm afraid I've got rather a weakness, and some people would get a bit shirty about it, but not here. They let me play Behemoth all night, even past the music hours. (*He indicates the stereophonic gramophone*) That's him, of course. "Behemoth" means a great monster, you know. It's in the Bible.

DOREEN. What is it, then, a gramophone?

BOB. Stereo.

DOREEN. It looks lovely. Interesting, I mean.

BOB (*a new note of warmth and pride in his voice*) You should hear him. (*He rises and crosses to the machine*) Do you know anything about these animals?

DOREEN. I'm afraid not, no.

BOB. Well, I shan't bother you with technical names, then. But I can tell you this is really the best machine a chap of my means could possibly afford, anywhere in the world. Of course, if you want to spend thousands, it'd be different. (*With an uncontrollable burst of true enthusiasm, he is off on his hobby-horse*) Behemoth's a real marvel, I can tell you. Most big sets can't play properly below a certain level. You can't hear them properly, unless they blast you out of your seat. That's because they've got bad speakers. (*He moves up* C *and indicates the speakers*) These things. Most speakers have only got between five and seven per cent efficiency. These have got between fifteen to twenty. Wharfedale Speakers. They're the best. I'm sorry: I promised not to give you technical names. It's the music that counts, anyway, isn't it? (*With great warmth*) I'm glad you like music. (*He moves to the stool and sits*) I can't tell you how glad I am to know that. You know, last week I'd been watching you for ages before you dropped that programme. I was watching you all through the Bach: and you were so wrapped up in listening, so concentrating, there were wrinkles all over your face.

(DOREEN *looks at him, startled and displeased*)

(*He falters*) Well, I mean, they were very becoming—I love to see lines on people's faces. I mean, that's their life, isn't it? It's what's happened to them. Most girls you see have got so much powder and muck on, you can't tell anything's happened to them. You know, they're like eggs, their skins. Eggshells, I mean. You're different.

DOREEN. You mean I've got inner beauty.

BOB. Do I?

DOREEN. That's what a man told me once. Inner beauty. It was his way of saying he was off me.

BOB (*rising*) That's not what I mean at all. (*He moves down* R. *Desperately*) You know the really wonderful thing about this machine? You can turn it up as loud as you like and all you hear is the faintest hum. (*He switches it on*)

Listen, I'm going to turn it right up. (*He turns the volume control as far as it will go*) See?

DOREEN (*blankly*) Wonderful.

BOB (*switching off; happily*) You must have been listening to music for an awfully long time to like Bach. Most people come to him only after a bit. When I first started it was all the *Symphonie Pathetique* and *Swan Lake*. You know.

DOREEN (*who has heard of this*) Oh—yes.

BOB. That's why Ted calls me "Tchaik": it's short for Tchaikovsky. I was mad about his music once. I thought Bach was boring, like exercises. Then one day I was shaving—isn't it daft how things happen—I always play records when I'm shaving, or in the bath—and I'd put on one of the Brandenburgs, you know, the Fourth with two flutes, and suddenly—just suddenly—I heard what made it marvellous. It wasn't about love or victory, or those romantic things that change all the time. It was about things that don't change. D'you see what I mean?

(DOREEN *gives him a quick, tight smile, but says nothing*)

Anyway, would you like to hear one? I've got all six.

DOREEN. Lovely . . .

BOB. Good. (*He crosses to the stool and moves it down* C, *facing the speakers*) Well, if you wouldn't mind moving here, you'd enjoy it better. You'd be midway between the two speakers at just the right distance. Let me help you. (*He moves to* R *of Doreen and takes the "ashtray"*)

(DOREEN *rises, moves to the stool and sits on it, with her back to the audience*)

That's it. Now—behold. (*He removes the cover from the top shelf down* R, *revealing the rack of records*)

DOREEN (*impressed*) Help! Are all those yours?

BOB. Every one. (*He puts the cover on the floor down* R)

DOREEN. But you must spend all your pay on records.

BOB. Well, you've got to spend it on something, haven't you? Which Brandenburg would you like? Or maybe you'd prefer the Goldbergs? Or the Musical Offering?

DOREEN (*who has never heard of any of these*) You choose.

BOB. No, it's your pleasure, madame.

DOREEN. Well, to be frank, I don't know that much about it. That old stuff isn't really me.

BOB. You mean you prefer Modern?

DOREEN (*seeing a gleam of hope*) That's right. Modern.

BOB. What d'you like? Stravinsky? Shostakovich?

DOREEN. Well, I don't quite mean that.

BOB. You mean something more tuneful?

DOREEN. Yes.

BOB. Benjamin Britten. Like me. I think Britten's the greatest composer in the world. I mean, he writes tunes, and makes wonderful sounds you can understand, not just plink-plonk. I hate all that twelve-tone stuff, don't you? It's sort of not—human. I know what I'll play you. (*He grabs an album*) *Peter Grimes*. Decca's done the most marvellous recording of it ever. D'you know it?

DOREEN. I can't say I do.

BOB (*switching on the gramophone*) It's the greatest thing you ever heard. (*He takes the record from its sleeve and cleans it with a sponge*) It's all about this lonely fisherman who lives by himself, and the village hates him because he's different, and has dreams and visions about what life should be. He dreams about this girl, Ellen—someone to share his life, you know, only he's not very good at expressing himself. (*He puts the record on the turntable*) In the end the village turns against him and accuses him of killing his apprentice. There's a sort of manhunt at night—people calling and shouting, hurrying in with lanterns. They make up a posse, you know: it's terrifying.

(BOB *starts the record towards the end of the great lynch chorus in Act Three*)

It's like a rising sea, getting wilder and wilder, up and up and up till it suddenly bursts over the town. I think it's the most marvellous thing I ever heard. Listen. (*He turns up the volume and listens to it, entranced, beating time to its hurtling rhythm and mouthing the words, which he clearly knows*)

(DOREEN *watches Bob with something much less like involvement: she obviously detests the music.* BOB *has put it on very loudly: it becomes quite deafening as it boils up into the great shouts of "Peter Grimes"! punctuated by silence)*

(He explains in a hushed voice) That's his name—"Peter Grimes". They all just stand there and call it. Sssh!

(The chorus yells "Grimes!" then there is a brief silence)

(He sings) "Peter Grimes!"

(TED enters from the kitchen with three soup bowls on a tray)

TED *(facetiously)* Did someone call me?

(DOREEN laughs and rises)

(He sets the bowls out on the table) Turn it down, for God's sake, or you'll have the neighbours in. *(He bangs the tray as a gong)* Come on, dinner up. *(To Doreen)* Madame! *(He indicates the chair above the table)*

DOREEN. Ooh! Lovely. *(She sits above the table)*

(BOB, his face set, stops the gramophone)

TED *(putting the tray against the wall L)* *Potage a la* Heinz. *Champignon!* Note that g-n sound, that's pronouncing it proper. Followed by lamb chops *a la* Ted Veasey.

(DOREEN laughs delightedly. BOB very elaborately switches off the set, puts the record in its sleeve and lays it on the machine. His movements are slow and mechanical. TED goes into the kitchen and returns with a plate of sliced Hovis)

Hey, Tchaik, stop fussing with that damn thing, and come and be host. It's your party, isn't it? *(He puts the plate on the table. To Doreen)* Now, take a nice slice of Hovis, my dear, it gives body to the soup!

(BOB moves to the stool to R of the table, and sits)

(He goes into the kitchen and returns with the bottle of wine) And have a fill-up on the rosé. That's it. *(He pours wine for Doreen and himself, then puts the bottle on the table)* Here's to you!

(BOB lifts his empty glass pointedly)

(He pours a drink for Bob) And you, chum!

BOB (*responding quietly to the toast*) Thank you. To you.
(*He drinks, keeping his eyes lowered*)

(TED *puts down his glass, goes into the kitchen and returns
with a saucepan of hot soup and a ladle*)

TED. You know, how you can stand that stuff, I'll never
know. Opera! How so-called intelligent people can listen
to it I just can't imagine. (*He serves soup into each bowl*) I
mean, who ever heard of people singing what they've got
to say? (*He sings to the tune of the Toreadors' song in "Carmen"*)
"Will you kindly pass the bread?" "Have a bowl of soup?"
"*Champignon.*" "I must go and turn the gas off." (*He puts
the saucepan in the kitchen and returns to the living-room*) Well,
for heaven's sake! If that's not a bloody silly way to go on,
excuse language, I don't know what is. I wish someone
would explain it to me, honest. I mean, I'm probably just
dead ignorant. (*He sits* L *of the table*)
BOB (*very quietly*) You are.

(TED *looks at Bob in surprise.* BOB *has never said anything
like this before.* BOB *looks at Ted with calm contempt. There
is a brief pause.* DOREEN *looks anxiously from one to the other*)

TED. Come on. Drink up before it gets cold. (*He taps his
bowl with his spoon*)

(*All three lift their spoons. They freeze. The* LIGHTS *fade
leaving only a pin-spot on Bob's face. The following dialogue
is heard through the loudspeakers from a tape-recording*)

DOREEN. Lovely soup. Is it mushroom?
TED. Of course not—it's toadstool.
DOREEN. Oh, you are awful! It's a nice flavour.
TED. Well, let's say it shows willing, anyway. Warms
you up on a cold night, like some others I could men-
tion.

(*The recording revolves into high-pitched gabble.* BOB *puts
down his spoon and drinks off an entire glass of wine, quickly
He picks up his spoon again, and freezes*)

DOREEN. Ooh, lovely! Chops!
TED. D'you like 'em?
DOREEN. They're my favourite, actually—chops—they

always were, ever since I was small. I always used to like the way there was a meaty bit in the middle of the fatty bit.

TED (*dirtily*) Yes, I know what you mean. Here's some peas to go with them . . .

(*There is more high-pitched gabble.* BOB *takes some more wine and drinks it, then freezes again*)

DOREEN. Ooh, lovely! Peaches!
TED. Yellow cling.
DOREEN. What's that?
TED. Their name.
DOREEN. It isn't.
TED. It is—yellow cling peaches. Say, what a name for your Chinese girl-friend. Yellow Cling Peach.

(DOREEN *laughs*)

DOREEN. Did you cook all that yourself?
TED. Every scrap.
DOREEN. That's wonderful. All the boys I've met don't do anything like that.
TED. I'll bet all the boys you've met don't do anything—full stop.
DOREEN. Pardon?
TED. Nothing. What time is it, then? (*Louder*) What time is it, then? What time is it, then?

(*The last line is recorded with an echo. The recording ends. The* LIGHTS *come up, but at a lower key. It is one hour later. The day has almost gone*)

BOB. Nine o'clock.

(*They lower their spoons and resume the scene*)

TED (*to Doreen*) Some more vino, then?
DOREEN. I don't mind if I do.
TED (*picking up the bottle*) Well, what d'you know? There isn't any. Tchaik's taken it all.
DOREEN (*giggling*) I thought he didn't drink.
TED (*posh*) Not on an empty stomach. (*To Bob*) You certainly make up for it on a full one.
DOREEN. Like my dad. Only that's cos he's got an ulcer. He can drink with his meal, but not before. If he drinks

before, it's murder. He's chewed the carpet before now. Once he tored a lump out of the fringe. Honest.

BOB. Poor chap.

DOREEN. Yes. He suffers terribly with it. Well, of course, he's a worrier. A natural worrier. He worries about everything.

TED. Does he worry about you?

DOREEN (*a little stiffly*) He's got nothing to worry about in that department.

TED. No?

DOREEN. No. I mean politics. Things like that. The way the world's going. I think his ulcer started to grow the day he was appointed to be branch secretary of the union.

TED. Well, that's enough to worry anybody. He's a union man, then?

DOREEN (*proudly*) All his life.

TED. Well, good luck to him.

DOREEN (*indignantly*) What d'you mean?

TED. I'm a Tory myself and I don't care who knows it. Bloody unions. If you ask me, they're doing their best to ruin the country.

DOREEN. That's just stupid.

BOB. Yes, I agree.

TED. You can shut up. You didn't even vote at the last election. Wherever you look you come back to the same thing. The unions. Always at the bottom of everything, the unions, demanding, demanding all the time. No settling day. Give them one thing, they want another, and another, and another till we're all bust—which we pretty nearly are now. The unions. They make me bloody sick!

DOREEN. Well, I don't agree with you.

TED. Well, of course you don't agree. What do you know about economics? About the real laws that govern industry? Nothing. What do you care? Damn all! Well?

DOREEN (*cowed*) Well—I don't know.

TED. 'Course you don't know.

DOREEN. Well, all the same . . .

TED. What?

DOREEN. My dad can remember the time when he had to fight to get twopence halfpenny a week.

TED. Your dad.

DOREEN. Yes, my dad.

TED. And how old a gentleman would he be, may one ask?

DOREEN. Well, he's getting on now.

TED. How old?

DOREEN. Sixty-one.

TED. Well, there you are then. (*He rises, crosses to the chest of drawers, takes a cigarette from the box, and lights it*) That's all in the past, isn't it? Of course the unions were O.K. then: that was the bad old days. But it's become a cause now: the union right or wrong. Eh, it's all so old-fashioned, the bosses against the workers. I can tell you one thing: if the unions are going to run this country, I'm moving out. (*He moves up* C) Because the rate they're going, they're going to bankrupt it completely and utterly inside ten years. Get the coffee, Tchaik. I'm worn out.

(BOB, *slightly tipsy, rises, goes into the kitchen and puts the kettle on the stove*)

(*To Doreen*) Come on, give a hand, luv. (*He sings to the tune of "Toreador"*) "That really was a very lovely meal—pass me the mats."

(DOREEN *gets the tray and helps* TED *to stack everything from the table*)

DOREEN. (*singing*) "The knives and forks and spoons ..."

(*They both giggle.*
BOB *comes from the kitchen*)

TED (*singing*) "Where is the tray—pom, pom, ti pom—leave the flowers . . ." (*He hands the loaded tray to Bob*) You've gone very quiet. Are you all right?

BOB. I'm fine. (*He takes the tray into the kitchen*)

TED (*picking up the vase*) It's all that wine.

(DOREEN *folds the cloth*)

(*To Doreen*) Did you know alcohol is what they call a depressant? (*He replaces the vase on the table*)

DOREEN. No.

TED. That's something most people don't know. Most people think it's a stimulant, but they're wrong. Not in the long run, it isn't.

DOREEN. You know a lot, don't you? I like people who know things. (*She moves* RC)

(TED *closes the kitchen door so Bob will not hear*)

TED. Well, there's no good being an ignoramus, is there? You know things, you get on. (*He moves to* L *of her*) Why don't you make yourself comfortable?

DOREEN. Thanks. (*She collects her handbag, crosses to the chest of drawers and puts the bag on them*)

(TED *closes the curtains at the window to the kitchen*)

That was a smashing dinner.

TED (*crossing to the stool*) Glad madame liked it.

DOREEN. I did, very much. You are clever. (*She lifts her skirt and pulls up her stocking*)

TED. Oh, *ce ne fais rien!* (*He picks up the cushions from the stool and tosses them on to the bed*) How d'you like Tchaik?

DOREEN (*without enthusiasm*) He's nice. (*She takes out her compact and attends to her make-up*)

TED. Certainly is, and a very good son to his old mother, which is more than you are, I bet. I mean—daughter.

DOREEN (*turning to face him*) My mother's dead, smarty. And for your information, I look after my dad, which I bet is more than you do.

TED (*moving to* L *of her*) Me? I look after Number One.

DOREEN. Yes: I bet!

TED. Well, the way I see it, I'm enough to look after. I haven't got time to take on anyone else. (*He makes a quick movement with his right hand to his breast pocket*)

(DOREEN *flinches*)

(*He takes out a comb and combs his hair*) Anyway, Tchaik's lucky: his old lady's in Warrington. Anyone can be a good son to someone living in Warrington. You go down there, have a couple of days, high tea, eggs and chips, quick kiss and you're away. Now me, my people live practically on the doorstep. Hounslow. Well, that's different, isn't it? You're flipping right, it is. "Why can't you live at home?" they say. (*He puts his comb in his pocket*) Who the devil wants to? "You can have your own room," they say. My own

room! I should just like to see me using my room for—
well, for what I use a room. Am I being crude?

DOREEN. I think you are, yes. (*She moves to the armchair and sits, leaving her bag on the chest of drawers*)

TED. Tsk, tsk, tsk, tsk! Dear me! You'll have to take me as you find me, then, won't you?

DOREEN. I'm not sure I find you very nice.

TED. No?

DOREEN. No.

TED. Well, that depends on what you're looking for, doesn't it?

DOREEN. Pardon?

TED. I find you smashing. I do, honest. I bet there's a lot of fun in you, once you loosen up.

(DOREEN *looks at him, startled*)

Oh, I don't mean that way. I don't know what you think of me.

DOREEN. Do you care?

TED. 'Course I do.

DOREEN. Well, if you're like most boys, your mind's on just one thing.

TED. Well, I'm not like most boys. I'm me. And my mind's on lots of things. What's *your* mind on, most of the time? That's when you're not looking after dad or going to Prom Concerts? What's with that, anyway? I don't get it. You're not the concerty type.

DOREEN (*rising*) You're Mr Know-all, aren't you? (*She moves c and faces Ted*)

TED. Well, are you?

DOREEN. No, as a matter of fact, I was given a ticket by a girl friend. She couldn't go, and it seemed silly to waste it. (*She indicates the kitchen*) Now he thinks I'm a music lover, and know about Bach and everything. Actually it was ever so boring. I realized I shouldn't have said "Yes" to him for tonight as soon as he asked me.

TED. What made you?

DOREEN. Well, I don't know. I don't get out that much. And he was very nice. Very courteous.

TED. I bet.

DOREEN. A blooming sight more better-mannered than what you are.

TED. Well, who's denying it? Tchaik's always had manners. He's one of Nature's gentlemen.

DOREEN. You're wicked, you know. You really are.

TED. I mean it. He's a good boy. He wouldn't hurt a fly—and that's not because he's a fly himself, either. Because he isn't. He's got feelings inside him I wouldn't know anything about—and you, neither.

DOREEN. Thanks.

TED. I mean it. Real deep feelings. They're no use to him, of course. They're in his way. If you ask me, you're better off without that dreamy bit.

DOREEN. What d'you mean?

TED. Dreams. Visions.

DOREEN. You mean he sees things?

TED. 'Course not.

DOREEN. What, then?

TED. Well, he has ideas about perfect women. He's got one about you.

DOREEN. He hasn't.

TED. He has. Why d'you think you're here? How many girls do you think he's ever asked here?

DOREEN. I dunno.

TED. One. (*He spells it*) W-O-N. And she looked like the back of a bus. (*He crosses to her*)

DOREEN. Well, what's he want with me, then?

TED. Nothing. You're a vision. You've got a long neck like Venus coming out of the sea.

DOREEN. Who?

TED. He thinks you're the dead spit of her. (*He goes to the head of the bed, takes down the picture of Venus, brings it and shows it to Doreen*)

DOREEN. Oh. I haven't got a long neck like that.

TED. I know you haven't. Yours is the standard size, but he won't leave it at that. He's got to stretch it a bit. A long neck's a sign of a generous nature.

DOREEN. He's a bit nutty, isn't he?

TED. Not really.

DOREEN. I think he is. When he was talking about that record his eyes went all glary.

TED. Oh, that's nothing. Just the old Celtic Twilight in him. (*He replaces the picture crookedly on its hook*)

DOREEN. Twilight?

TED. Just a phrase.

DOREEN. You don't half have a way of putting things. You've got a gift for words, haven't you?

TED (*moving to the armchair*) Always had. Words, languages. It's why I took up French in the evenings.

DOREEN (*admiringly*) I like that.

TED (*sitting on the armchair*) Do you? Most people would say it was getting above myself. Then most people just don't count. They've got no drive, no ambition, nothing. I bet your dad had some go in him when he was young.

DOREEN. He still does.

TED. Course. They do, those old ones. They've got guts. Not pampered and spoilt like the kids today.

DOREEN. That's what he says.

TED (*sarcastic*) I bet.

DOREEN. What d'you mean?

TED (*hastily*) Well, I mean, he's all right. You're a lucky girl.

DOREEN. Me?

TED. To have a sensible old dad like that. You should meet mine. Mr Alcohol, one-nine-three-four. That's when he decided draught Guinness was the secret of life. Well, not decided exactly. He hasn't decided anything since he married my mum, and then he was pushed into it by me, if you see what I mean. . . . She's not much better, mind.

DOREEN. Your mum?

TED. I was a middle-aged slave—or Ten Years in a Bingo Hall! That's when she goes out at all. Mostly she stays in with the telly and a quarter bottle of Gordons. Am I shocking you?

DOREEN. Of course not.

TED (*seriously*) Most people make me sick. They talk about us being sick. It's them. The old ones. Sick, sick, bloody sick! When I say I don't want a room at home, it's cos I can't stand being with yobs. People who've given up. No—who've never started. They don't want to know. Not because they're old. Because they never did. Your dad

C

sounds different. Like you. I could never be serious about
a girl who was one of that lot.

DOREEN. I don't think you could be serious about
anyone.

TED. That's where you're wrong. That's where you are
utterly and completely wrong. You don't know me. I
could be very serious about someone, if she helped me go
places . . . She'd have to have a bit of fun in her, too,
mind.

(*Dance music is heard*)

Do you dance?

DOREEN. I do a bit, yes.

(TED *stands and takes from his pocket a transistor radio*)

Oh! That's smashing.

TED (*starting to dance*) I bet you're a real hot pot of coffee
on the floor.

DOREEN. Pardon?

TED. I bet you swing, Doreen girl. I bet you get really
with it.

(BOB, *preparatory to bringing in the coffee, noiselessly opens
the kitchen door and stands listening*)

You ever been to the *Mecca?*

DOREEN. No.

TED. You'd like that. It's really nice. Classy, you know.
None of that cave-man stuff. Of course, if you do a bit of
a wriggle, no-one exactly minds.

(DOREEN *laughs*)

I'll take you there if you like.

DOREEN. When?

TED. Any time. You name it.

DOREEN. Well, I'm not sure I'd like it.

TED. 'Course you would. It's good clean fun, as they
say. Honest—none of that touch-you-up and look the other
way. Straight up. What about next Friday? They have
a Late Night Special Fridays, eight to one.

(BOB *withdraws*)

DOREEN. No, next Friday I'm busy. (*She crosses behind him watching him "Twist"*)

TED (*not to be put off*) Friday after, then? (*He stops dancing*) Well?

DOREEN (*suddenly capitulating*) All right. (*She crosses to c*)

TED. Good. You'd better give me your phone number, then.

DOREEN. No, I'll meet you there.

TED. I can't have you going there on your own. I'll have to pick you up. That's if you don't live in Norwood, or some lousy place like that.

DOREEN. No. Putney.

TED. You're lucky. That's just inside my cruising area. (*He switches off the transistor. Seriously*) You're all right, you know. (*He moves to R of her*) You've got it.

DOREEN (*sitting on the stool*) Got what?

TED. Oh, that certain something. It used to be called carriage.

DOREEN. Carriage?

TED. People call it class nowadays, but it's not the same thing.

DOREEN. Carriage . . . What a nice word.

(BOB *comes from the kitchen with a tray of coffee for three*)

(*He sees Bob. With false breeziness*) Well—I'm away.

(BOB *crosses to c*)

I'll just have my coffee, and *allez*. (*He takes a cup of coffee and crosses to the chest of drawers*) Love you and leave you.

DOREEN (*disappointed*) Oh! Why? (*She takes a cup of coffee*)

TED. Duty calls. (*In an "executive" voice*) All that work I took home from the office, clamouring for my attention.

DOREEN. Go on!

TED. Well, that's my story, and I'm stuck with it. No sugar?

BOB. Sorry. (*He puts the tray on the table and goes into the kitchen*)

(TED *picks up a cigarette packet, puts his cup on the chest of drawers and crosses to Doreen*)

TED. Ciggy?

DOREEN. No, thank you.

TED (*offering her the packet*) Go on.

DOREEN. No, really.

TED (*sotto voce*) Telephone.

DOREEN. What?

TED (*through clenched teeth*) Number.

DOREEN (*understanding*) Oh. Got a pen? (*She takes the cigarette packet*)

(BOB *comes from the kitchen.* TED *is about to give Doreen a pen, sees Bob and crosses to the chest of drawers*)

(*Very flustered*) It's lovely coffee.

BOB. It's only powdered. (*He puts a bowl of sugar on the table, then sits* L *of the table*)

DOREEN. Well, you must have a way with it, then. It tastes like it's really ground. Like it's been perking for hours in one of those things. Really. Continental, you know. (*She becomes aware of the cigarette packet in her hand*) Can I have the little girl's room?

BOB (*rising, moving to the door down* L *and opening it*) It's out on the landing.

(DOREEN *rises, puts her coffee on the table, crosses to the chest of drawers, picks up her handbag, takes the pen from Ted, then crosses to the door down* L)

I'll show you.

DOREEN. It's all right. I can find it.

(DOREEN *exits down* L. BOB *closes the door then leans against it, looking at Ted*)

TED (*after a pause*) Well, it's nine-thirty. I'm off. Count ten and I'll be gone. (*He moves to the table*) I wish I was in your shoes. I do, honest. Not going home to my empty bed-sit. I tell you, mate, your card is definitely marked. We're frying tonight. What's the matter? (*He puts sugar in his coffee*)

BOB. Nothing.

TED. Are you all right?

BOB. That's like "How do you do?" isn't it? There's no answer expected. (*He goes into the kitchen*)

TED. What? Now pull yourself together, Tchaik. Don't start that pit-a-pat going again. What have you got to worry about? I've chatted her, and she told me she likes you a lot. She thinks you're the most courteous man she ever met. That's her actual word for you—courteous. If you ask me, it's time you stopped being so flipping courteous. Get off your knees. This is a girl, that's all. Not a goddess. And no girl wants to be worshipped, whatever she may tell you. You just give her a shove off her pedestal, you'll find she won't exactly resent it.

BOB (*coming from the kitchen*) Go home, Ted. (*He opens the door down* L)

(TED *crosses the room in silence to the door, then suddenly slams it violently*)

TED. I am going home. The only reason I'm still here at nine-thirty-two belting back my coffee, is because you seem in dire danger of jeopardizing your immediate succulent prospects. And that upsets me. It makes me feel I've wasted my time. After all, I've gone to no little trouble to ensure the success of this enterprise.

BOB. What?

TED. Well, haven't I? What do you think I've been doing here all evening?

BOB. I don't know. You tell me.

TED. What's the matter with you? You've been hitting the vino a bit, haven't you? You asked me here tonight to set it up for you. And that's what I've done. Just that. I've knocked myself out for you this past two hours, breaking her in nice and easy. Flowers on the table—chilled wine before din—the old sexy dance afterwards to get her in the proper receptive mood. To say nothing of cooking the meal itself. I'm not looking for thanks, mate.

BOB (*moving to* L *of the table*) Ted, what does it feel like to be a stupid, selfish, ignorant clod?

(*There is a very long pause.* BOB *crosses slowly to* C *below the table* TED *remains by the door*)

TED. Ignorant? That's twice in one night. That's a bit too much even for me. Ignorant. Selfish. That's lovely, that is. Selfish . . . I didn't have to come here tonight, you know. I could have gone to one of a dozen places. I didn't have to be doing here. I could have gone up to the Mecca, the bowling alley, any place. But I didn't. I came here to help out my mate Tchaik, who had the pit-a-pats, and couldn't manage on his own. And that's all the thanks I get. That's all the thanks I bloody get! (*He crosses* R *for his hat*) Well, I'll know better next time, won't I? I'll know better than to ever try and help someone else. (*He puts on his hat*)

(BOB *has remained standing, not looking at him, shamefaced*)

BOB. Help. You don't know what that is. Oh, you do your best as you see it. But what if that's nothing, what you see. You'll have lived in vain.

(*There is a small pause*)

TED. You're sloshed, Tchaik. I'll excuse it because of that.

BOB. Excuse it? I don't want excuse from you. Bloody you . . . (*Controlling himself*) Go home, Ted. You should never have come here in the first place.

(TED *puts on his sun-glasses. He whistles a few bars of* "*Toreador*", *then crosses to face Bob.*

DOREEN *enters down* L, *and stands down* L *of the table. Summoning up a jaunty exit* TED *pats Bob lightly on the shoulder, and exits down* L, *quickly, ignoring Doreen.* BOB *stands looking after him. The light fades a little as the sun goes. Night falls during the rest of the play*)

DOREEN. Where's he going?
BOB. Home.
DOREEN. Home?
BOB. Yes.
DOREEN. You mean he's not coming back?
BOB. I don't think so, no.
DOREEN (*unable to take it in*) You mean he's just gone off like that, without even saying good night?

BOB. Well, yes . . . He doesn't set much store on things like good night. He had work to do at home, very urgent. Remember, he did say.

DOREEN. Did he?

BOB. Yes. And he won't let anything stand in the way of his work. That's what's called Drive.

DOREEN. Have you two had words, then?

BOB. No.

DOREEN. What about?

BOB. Nothing.

DOREEN. Was it over me, then?

BOB. Of course not.

(DOREEN *crosses* L, *opens the door and goes out on to the landing to look for Ted*)

BOB (*calling after her*) I mean—why should it be?

DOREEN (*off*) I don't know, I'm sure.

BOB. I've poured your coffee.

DOREEN. I think that's the rudest thing I've ever heard of.

BOB. It's getting cold.

DOREEN (*coming back on stage*) Ever, in my whole life.

BOB. He didn't mean it that way?

DOREEN (*closing the door*) Well, what way did he mean it, then?

BOB. How should I know? . . . (*Pause. Sitting on the stool* C) It's all my fault, really. I had too much to drink, and I can't really carry it, you see. Did you know that alcohol isn't really a stimulant at all, it's a depressant?

DOREEN. I know. I heard. (*She sits in the chair* L *of the table*)

BOB (*smiling*) He means well, you know. He's good-hearted. Much more than me, really, if the truth were known. I'm not exactly fond of him, but you get attached out of habit. He knows a lot, and he's always laughing. We have a lot of laughs in the office, really.

DOREEN (*without enthusiasm*) That's good.

BOB. Yes.

DOREEN. What office would that be, then?

BOB. Import—export.

DOREEN. I mean the actual address.

BOB. Address?

DOREEN. Of your office.

BOB. Why?

DOREEN. No reason . . . I just asked.

BOB. I see.

(DOREEN *has been fiddling with the cigarette packet and pencil half in and half out of her bag. Now she drops them both into it, and shuts it. A pause*)

DOREEN. It must be nice having a friend in the same office. I mean, someone you're close to.

BOB. That depends what you mean by close, doesn't it?

DOREEN. Pardon? (*She puts the pen and packet into her bag*)

BOB. We've been in the same room, but that doesn't make you close. No-one in the office is close. That's what's wrong with them. You don't get to know anyone. But you're different. You know people at once, without having to try. I could tell that as soon as I saw you.

DOREEN. I don't know about that.

BOB. Oh, it's true. It's the obvious thing about you. Now, what would you say about me first sight. That I was a clerk?

DOREEN. Not specially, no.

BOB. Then what? Because I don't know. I suppose that's the point of education. Finding out who you really are. I never had that. (*He rises and moves* R)

DOREEN. Why not?

BOB. Well, when I could have done, I didn't want it. I hated school. (*He picks up the "Peter Grimes" record, puts it in the album and puts the album on the rack*)

DOREEN. So did I.

BOB. I hated it so much, I took the first job that came along.

DOREEN. What did you come down here for?

BOB. When dad died I came south. If I could start again, I'd *make* myself *study*. (*He moves up* C)

DOREEN. Well, you could if you wanted. You're still young. You could go to night school.

BOB. No.

DOREEN. Why not? Your friend does.

BOB (*moving to* R *of the table*) Well, of course, he's got drive. You lot go on about drive, but you can't have drive without enjoying your work. Now Ted does. When he leaves the office he's as fresh as a daisy, but when I come home I've hardly got the energy to grill a chop, let alone pick up a French book; and what have I done? Filled in about sixty invoices. What a way to spend your day: and some of those people have been doing it for thirty years. Taking endless dictation. Typing thousands of meaningless letters. Tenth of the inst. and eleventh ultimo. C.I.F.— E. and O.E. Thanking you in anticipation. Your esteemed order. Are you going to spend the rest of your life typing nonsense? Top copy and two carbons?

DOREEN. Well, like I say, we haven't got much choice, have we?

BOB (*kneeling on the stool and facing her*) Yes, we have. We must have. We weren't born to do this. Eyes. Complicated things like eyes, weren't made by God just to see columns of twopence-halfpennies written up in a ledger. Tongues. Good grief, the woman next to me in the office even sounds like a typewriter. A thin, chipped old typewriter, always clattering on about what Miss Story said in Accounts and Mr Burnham said back. It's awful! Do you know how many thousands of years it took to make anything so beautiful, so feeling, as your hand? People say I know something like the back of my hand, but they don't know their hands. They wouldn't recognize a photograph of them. Why? Because their hands are anonymous. They're just tools for filling invoices, turning lathes round. They cramp up from picking slag out of moving belts of coal. If that's not blasphemy, what is? I'll tell you something really daft. Some nights when I come back here I give Behemoth a record for his supper. That's the way I look at him sometimes, feeding off discs, you know. And I conduct it. If it's a Concerto I play the solo part, running up and down the keyboard, doing the expressive bits, everything. I imagine someone I love is sitting out in the audience watching; you know, someone I want to admire me. Anyway, it sort of frees things inside me. At great moments I feel shivery all over. It's marvellous to feel shivery like that. What I want to know is, why can't I feel that in my work? Why can't I—oh, I don't know—feel bigger? There's something in me I know that's big. That can be excited, anyway. And that must mean I can excite other people, if only I knew what way. I never met anyone to show me that way.

(*There is a pause*)

DOREEN. Well.

(*Pause*)

BOB. Well. So.

(*Pause*)

DOREEN. I suppose I must be going then.
BOB. Yes.

(DOREEN *rises*)

You're quite pretty, you know.
DOREEN. Thank you. (*She moves towards the door, down* L)
BOB (*crossing to her*) I mean very pretty, really . . . Please stay just a little longer.
DOREEN. I'm afraid I can't. My dad'll be worrying about me. (*She takes her coat from the hook*)
BOB. Does he worry that much about you?
DOREEN. Yes, he's a natural worrier.
BOB. Well, how about one more record before you go?
DOREEN (*putting on the coat*) Worries about everything.
BOB. One for the road, as they say.
DOREEN. Old people always do, don't they?
BOB (*desperately*) Something more tuneful and luscious! Madam Butterfly! . . . (*He runs to* R, *takes the record from the rack and switches on the gramophone*) D'you know the Love Duet? You'll like that. I know it's awfully corny, but I do love all that fudgy sort of music. At least I have great sort of cravings for it. (*He takes the record from its sleeve*) Like I suppose some people have for chocolates. (*He drops the sleeve on the floor and holds out the record*) Try a bit.

DOREEN (*opening the door*) Well, really, it is getting rather late.

BOB (*moving appealingly towards her*) It only takes three minutes.

DOREEN (*closing the door*) Well—all right.

(BOB *crosses to the gramophone and puts the record on the turntable: the start of the Love Duet from "Madam Butterfly". We hear the quiet orchestral music before "Vogliatemi bene, un bene piccolino"*)

BOB. You know what's happening, don't you? Pinkerton —that's the American sailor—has married this Japanese girl in spite of her family and the priests and everybody. This is the first time they are alone together.

MIME

There now ensues a six-minute sequence in which not a word is spoken. The following is a movement by movement description of what was done at the first production. It need not be slavishly followed. The mood must be tender, at times comic and even absurd—but always real. It must never suggest a revue sketch. And it must end in humiliation and embarrassment for both.

The LIGHTS *dim, except for the area* C, *around the gramophone and around the armchair. As the singing starts,* BOB *stares at the turntable:* DOREEN *remains by the door. After a moment he turns and motions her to sit in the armchair. Gingerly* DOREEN *complies. She sits.* BOB *starts conducting the music: she stares at him, and he becomes self-conscious, stops, shyly crosses above her to the stool* C, *and sits. She relaxes, pushing her shoes off and stretching.* BOB, *plucking up a little courage, moves the stool a little nearer to her. She looks at him: he moves it yet nearer. She picks up her handbag from the floor at her left and deliberately moves it to the right side. He now moves the stool close to her left side.* DOREEN *smiles, looks approvingly at the turntable, and herself begins to conduct, looking round at the speakers and mouthing, "Lovely!" As she listens the boy touches her sleeve. She turns and he abruptly turns the motion into a gesture miming: "Would you like a cigarette?" Eagerly, she nods.* BOB *rises, crosses to the chest of drawers, picks up the cigarette box and matches.* DOREEN *takes a cigarette and* BOB *puts the box on the floor. He opens the box of matches, but he is looking at her and the box is upside down: the matches spill. Together they pick them up from the carpet, and then he strikes one and lights her cigarette. Fascinated by her prettiness, he stares at her: the flame of the match burns between them until she gently blows it out. They stare at one another. She offers him a puff of her cigarette. He declines—then accepts—takes a puff: then a big one and chokes a little. He takes her hand and begins to study it with intense concentration.*

Suddenly DOREEN *is sorry for the boy. She closes her eyes and lowers her face to be kissed. He looks at her, uncertain what to do. Slowly, hardly daring, he raises himself from the floor to kiss her. He nearly does so, but suddenly she thinks she has burnt her coat with the cigarette in her left hand. She wets her finger and rubs the spot.* BOB *jumps up, gets the plaster-lid "ashtray" from the chest of drawers, and hands it to her, again kneeling* R *of her. All is well with her coat: she adopts her former pose of invitation. This time* BOB *raises himself and is about to kiss her lips: at the last moment switches to her forehead. She opens her eyes a little impatiently and tugs at the collar of her coat. It is a little hot, isn't it? She undoes the buttons and tape of her coat.* BOB *rises to help her out of the coat, which he places over the back of her chair.* DOREEN *rises, straightens her dress, and putting her right leg under her, sits and again offers her lips. This time* BOB *responds more confidently: he kisses her. Then liking it, he tries again, sitting on the arm of the chair and pressing her back. The eagerness of his response surprises and alarms the girl. She struggles to free herself, pushing herself forward so that* BOB *falls down behind her and is trapped across the arms of the chair behind her back.* DOREEN, *sitting on her right leg, finds she cannot move. She struggles to free it—then rises precipitately and moves to* R *of the table.* BOB *rises and follows her. He is rumpled and desperate: he is no longer listening to the passionate, undisturbable lovers singing so ecstatically on the gramophone. Slowly, his mind full of how* TED *would cope under these circumstances, he begins to follow her round the room: as slowly she retreats up stage, backwards, to the corner of the room. She stumbles back on to the bed. The boy falls softly on top of her, and tries with a muddled gentleness*

*to show her passion. She tries haplessly to avoid him. Finally
she pushes him away and moves away from him down C.*

BOB *stares after her. Then he, too, gets up and comes towards
her with a gesture at once desperate and supplicating. Puccini's
Love Duet rises to its climax. As the final climactic chord crashes
over the room,* DOREEN *slaps his face—then, horrified, takes it
between her hands, trying to recall the blow. He moves away
from her across the stage,* R: *she from him,* L. *By the chest of
drawers he turns and appeals to her, saying he is sorry. We
cannot hear this because of the music. He slowly goes to the
turntable and lifts the stylus just before the quiet closing music
of the duet finishes.*

BOB. I'm sorry.
DOREEN. That's all right. (*She crosses to* RC, *sits on the
stool, puts on her shoes and picks up her handbag*)
BOB. No, no, it isn't. It isn't at all. Actually, you see,
I've brought you here under false pretences. I should never
have asked you. You see, I didn't really tell you everything
about myself. That was wrong of me. Please forgive me.
DOREEN. What d'you mean?
BOB. Well, you see, actually I'm engaged. (*He picks up
the cigarette box and matches*)
DOREEN. Engaged?
BOB. Yes. To be married.
DOREEN (*really surprised*) *You* are?
BOB (*defiantly*) Yes. Yes. So I shouldn't have asked you
here. I'm sorry.

(DOREEN *stares at* BOB, *who is not looking at her*)

DOREEN (*pointing to the photograph in the mirror*) Is that her?
BOB (*looking at the photograph*) Yes.
DOREEN. Can I see?

(BOB *goes to the mirror, takes down the photograph and hands
it to Doreen*)

She looks lovely.
BOB. Yes, very. That's really raven black hair. It's got
tints of blue in it. You can't really judge from a photo.
DOREEN. What's her name?

BOB. Er—Lavinia. It's rather an unusual name, isn't it? Lavinia. I think it's rather distinguished.

DOREEN. Yes, it is.

BOB. Like her. She's distinguished. She's got a way with her. Style, you know. It's what they used to call carriage.

(DOREEN *gives him a startled look*)

DOREEN. Carriage?

BOB. In the old days.

DOREEN. I see.

BOB (*taking the photograph from her and putting it on the chest of drawers*) Well—no harm done, I suppose.

DOREEN (*rising*) No, of course not.

BOB (*picking up her coat*) Here's your coat.

(DOREEN *looks at him, touched for the first time by a feeling of sympathy she cannot analyse.* BOB *helps* DOREEN *on with her coat*)

I wonder why I thought ocelot was a bird. I wasn't thinking of an ostrich. It was those pictures you see of ladies in Edwardian photos with long, traily feathers in their hats. Is there such a thing as an osprey?

DOREEN. I wouldn't know. (*With a smile*) It's not really ocelot, you know. It's lamb dyed. And it's not really cold enough for fur coats, anyway, is it, yet? I was showing off.

BOB. I'm glad you did.

(DOREEN *moves to the door down* L. BOB *overtakes her and opens the door*)

DOREEN. Well, it's been lovely.

BOB. For me, too.

DOREEN. I enjoyed the music. Really.

BOB. Did you?

DOREEN. Perhaps we'll meet again. At a concert or somewhere.

BOB. Yes.

DOREEN. I'm glad about your girl. She looks lovely.

BOB. She is.

(*They stare at one another, nervously*)

DOREEN. Well, good night. (*She moves to the door*)

BOB. Good night. (*He moves quickly to* R *of her*) Fabian and Carter.

DOREEN. Pardon?

BOB. The name of the firm. Where Ted works. You wanted to know it. Fabian and Carter. Bishopsgate two-four-three-seven. Good-bye.

DOREEN *gives Bob a quick smile and exits down* L. BOB *closes the door, switches on the light, turns and surveys the empty room, then walks aimless across it. He stops by the gramophone and puts the stylus on the record. We hear the first strains of "Madame Butterfly". He stands by it as it plays and looks down at the turning record. After a moment he crouches behind the turntable, lifts the stylus, then, with infinite slowness, staring at it, he moves the needle right across the record, then again across, making a terrible sound and damaging the record beyond repair. He puts the stylus on the record and "Madame Butterfly" is heard again, but now there is a deep scratch clicking the music, ruining it. BOB stares at it as it plays with an expressionless face. The* LIGHTS *slowly dim to Black-Out as—*

the CURTAIN *falls*

FURNITURE AND PROPERTY LIST

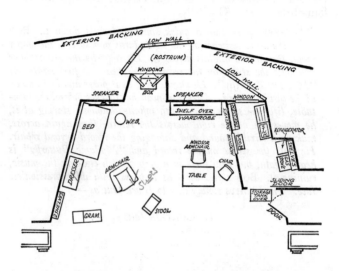

On stage: Shelves (down R)

    On top shelf: 64 record sleeves in racks and a red album of "Peter Grimes" with records

    On bottom shelf: assorted books. Set of 6 Fontana Pocket Library of Great Art, including book of Botticelli

Chest of drawers (R)

    On it: mirror, Bob's tie, Dimple Haig bottle containing 6d pieces, 2 boxes matches, small vase, cigarette box with plain and tipped cigarettes, lighter (not working), 3 books, alarm clock, bust of Beethoven, Olivier cigarette packet, brush and comb, record of *Madame Butterfly* in album

In drawer: pair of socks for Bob, tin of finger plasters

Bed. *On it:* mattress, bolster, 2 pillows, bedspread, 5 cushions, Bob's trousers

On wall R *of bed:* 6 assorted Classical Concert programmes, pasted on wall

On wall at head of bed: framed print for Botticelli's "Venus rising from the Sea"

On ceiling R *and* L *of window:* 2 stereo speakers (dummy)

On floor up C: waste-paper basket

On line across window: Bob's shirt on hanger

Under window: box

On roof wall: teacloth

Armchair (RC) *On it:* Bob's raincoat with unopened bottle of wine in pocket, pair of socks, one with hole

Under armchair: rug

Stool (down C)

L *of window:* shelf with bar and curtains on runners

    On shelf: case, pile of music magazines

    On bar: hangers with plastic mac, pin-striped suit, tweed jacket, 2 pair tweed trousers, spare hanger, Bob's blazer with cleaner's label on right sleeve and tag on back of collar

Curtains for window L

Light switch (L of kitchen door)

On door L: doorbell, hook with coat-hanger

Over kitchen door: water cistern

Table (LC) *In drawer:* tablecloth, 3 mats

Windsor armchair

Upright chair

Down R: stereophonic gramophone with practical turntable with wires to plug in wall down R and to the loud-speakers. Record-cleaning sponge in cellophane bag

On floor R *of gramophone:* 6 music magazines

Electric pendant C

On floor L *of armchair:* Bob's shoes

In kitchen:

    On R *wall inside doorway:* hook

    On floor: supermarket carrier bag with 3 lamb chops in cardboard tray covered with cellophane, tin of Heinz mushroom soup, tin of peas, tin of peaches, packet of sliced Hovis

Small table (R) *On it:* tray with jug of water, 3 glasses, 3 knives, 3 forks, 3 spoons, 3 paper serviettes

On shelves R: 2 enamel saucepans, colander, wire sieve, mixing bowl, 2 saucepan lids, enamel bowl

Hanging under back window: raffia shopping bag, carrier bag

Sink with draining-board. *In it:* enamel bowl

Over sink: Ascot (dummy), plate-rack with 4 tea plates, 2 breakfast plates, water tap (practical), tank of water behind flat, syphoned with rubber tube

Refrigerator

Gas stove. *On it:* saucepan with soup and ladle

On shelves L:

> *Top shelf:* enamel teapot, cheese grater, packet of borax, china teapot, milk saucepan
>
> *2nd shelf:* tin of instant coffee, jug of milk, 3 cups, 3 saucers, empty sugar bowl, packet of cube sugar, 3 teaspoons, box of eggs, tea caddy, plastic salad spoon, box of Beechams, tin of brewer's yeast, packet of birdseed
>
> *Bottom shelf:* 2 glasses, pink wine, 3 soup bowls, salt cellar, shaving mirror, pint bottle milk, ashtray, tea towel

On refrigerator: wooden tray, small round tray, tin opener, bottle of wine (half full—replica of full bottle in Bob's raincoat), sliced Hovis

Off stage: Transistor (TED)

Small bunch of sweet peas in tissue paper (TED)

Towel (BOB)

Dressing-gown. *In pocket:* wrist watch (BOB)

In kitchen: saucepan of hot soup with ladle (TED)

Tray with 3 cups of coffee (BOB)

Sugar basin (BOB)

Personal: TED: sun-glasses, comb, photograph, watch, Biro

DOREEN: handbag. *In it:* matches, lipstick, compact

LIGHTING PLOT

Property fittings required: pendant LC. Switch above door down L. A special spot is set for Bob when he is seated R of the table, and is used during the recorded dialogue. It is a pin-focus and lights his face only. Care should be taken there is no spill so that the other characters remain in the dark.

Interior. A bed-sitting-room. The same scene throughout

THE MAIN ACTING AREAS are L, LC, C, RC and R

THE APPARENT SOURCES OF LIGHT are, in daytime, windows up C and up L; and at night, a pendant light LC

To open: The stage in darkness

Cue 1	At rise of CURTAIN	(Page 1)
	Bring in general lighting for bright sunshine effect	
	Fitting off	
Cue 2	TED: ". . . before it gets cold."	(Page 22)
	Dim lights to BLACK-OUT except for spot on Bob	
Cue 3	TED: "What time is it, then?"	(Page 23)
	Bring up lights as Cue 1, but at a lower key for evening effect	
Cue 4	TED exits	(Page 34)
	Dim lights for twilight effect	
Cue 5	As record plays *Madame Butterfly*	(Page 39)
	Dim lighting except for the area C, around the gramophone and around the armchair	
Cue 6	During mime—after the kiss	(Page 40)
	Bring up lights L	

Cue 7	Bob switches on light *Snap in pendant* *Snap in covering lights*	(Page 43)
Cue 8	At end of Scene *Dim to* Black-Out	(Page 43)

EFFECTS PLOT

Cue 13	Bob lifts stylus	(Page 41)
	Stop music	
Cue 14	Bob starts gramophone	(Page 43)
	Music of "Madame Butterfly"	
Cue 15	Bob lifts stylus	(Page 43)
	Stop music	
Cue 16	Bob scratches record	(Page 43)
	Scratch effect	
Cue 17	Bob starts gramophone	(Page 43)
	Music of "Madame Butterfly" from damaged record	

Any character costumes or wigs needed in the performance of this play can be hired from CHARLES H. FOX LTD, 184 High Holborn, London W.C.1